OAK TREE MYSTERY

Book 4

Written by Jenny Phillips

Illustrations by Kessler Garrity

Cover Illustration by Brandon Dorman

Books in the Badger Hills Farm Series

TABLE OF CONTENTS

CHAPTER 1

Z OEY CLOSED HER EYES AND LISTENED TO the sounds around her: birds twittering in the trees, bees buzzing gently in the clumps of flowers nearby, pine boughs rushing in the breeze, and the stream gurgling softly. *Ah, the sounds of early spring*, Zoey thought as she sighed.

Leaving the little grove of trees close to her home, Zoey smiled as she strolled down the narrow asphalt lane. *I miss the crunch of gravel*, she thought. *But I love how easy it is for Mrs. Bastian to come over and visit now without having to drive her van here. She can just come right over in her wheelchair.*

"Zoey! Zoey!" Jessica's voice rang out from down the road. "I have a question!"

"What is it?" Zoey asked when Jessica reached her.

"Volleyball!" Jessica burst out. "My club volleyball team needs another player. Twin sisters on our team are suddenly moving, and another girl on our team broke a finger. We can't play unless we have one more person. We are in the championships and only have two games left. We really need you!"

Zoey frowned. "Well, thanks for thinking of me, but I don't play volleyball. In fact, I'm

not the sporty type at all!"

"Oh, you really should do it," Jessica pleaded. "We practice every Tuesday and Thursday at seven and have games Saturday mornings, so you would get two practices in before the first game. I'm sure you would learn quickly. I've told you before how much I love volleyball. It's so fun! You don't have to be amazing; all you have to do is try. And besides, we'd get to see each other even more often!"

Zoey laughed. "I don't think you took a breath between all those sentences. You're quite convincing. But I need to think about it. Can I let you know tomorrow?"

"Sure," Jessica said. "Have your mom text my mom with your answer. I have to run. I've got to babysit tonight."

4

And with that, Jessica was off, her braids swinging as she jogged back down the lane.

Continuing down the road, Zoey pondered the last few months. The fence around the farm was finished, and it was as beautiful as her family had hoped it would be. It also made Badger Hills Farm feel safe and secure against trespassers. *I hope it will help keep the animals safer too,* Zoey thought. Last month, before the fence was finished, a badger had been hit by a car on the street next to the farm.

In happier news, Sammy had successfully graduated from his dog training school and now obeyed Timothy's commands. The boy and dog were the best of friends. They had also rejoiced when Nanna Bell had returned home after caring for her injured brother.

Zoey's smile changed to a frown when she turned the corner and saw the barn looming before her. Once, she had been so excited for the barn to be finished so that she could bring Misty Toes and her foal from Mrs. Bastian's barn to her own barn. But now, the barn just reminded her that she was too scared to ride Misty Toes since she had fallen off.

Secretly, Zoey had felt angry at her horse—betrayed, even—since the fall. Yes, falling off the horse had hurt her body, and the staples in her head had been painful too, but her feelings were hurt more, and she didn't really understand why. She still did her duty every day: She fed Misty Toes and took care of her. But she didn't talk to and hug her horse like she used to.

A swirl of sadness moved through Zoey's heart as she shuffled into the barn and took care of the horses. She stood close to the stalls for a moment, watching Misty Toes's foal, who was quite big now.

I need to name her, Zoey thought. *It's way past time. I just can't think of a name!*

The foal cocked her head slightly and gazed into Zoey's eyes. In that moment, time seemed to stand still. Zoey felt a deep longing to connect with a horse again. She took a step forward and gently stretched her hand toward the foal.

Without warning, the walls began to rattle, and the earth rolled beneath her feet. Zoey fell hard.

It's an earthquake, she realized as a deep

grumble vibrated through the ground. Zoey quickly got out of the stall. Glass shattered. Zoey dropped to the ground, rolled to the side of the barn, and curled up with her hands over her head. All around were the terrible creaking and rattling of wood, the crashes of things falling to the ground, and the loud whinnies and neighs of the frightened horses. Zoey squeezed her eyes closed and tried to remain calm.

Thirty seconds seemed like an eternity. Finally, the ground became still, and the earthquake was over. Zoey uncurled herself and slowly stood up on shaking legs. Scanning her surroundings, she noticed that a window in the barn had broken and some wooden boards had fallen from the ceiling. Metal pails and

saddles that had been hanging on the wall were now scattered on the floor.

Misty Toes pranced in her stall, eyes rolling. Poor girl! She hadn't understood what was happening in the earthquake and must have been very scared. Zoey rushed to the horse and calmed her down with soft words and strokes. After a few moments, Misty Toes nuzzled Zoey's arm in a show of love. Zoey realized that the horse still trusted her and that she hadn't meant to hurt her before. With a full heart, Zoey threw her arms around her beloved horse. At that moment, she knew she had completely forgiven Misty Toes.

CHAPTER 2

FROM OUTSIDE THE BARN CAME THE pounding of feet. "Zoey! Zoey!" It was Zoey's dad, John. "Zoey, are you OK? Where are you?"

It had felt so good to hug Misty Toes, but it felt even better to be safe in her dad's warm embrace.

"I'm so relieved you're not hurt," John said. "Are the horses OK?"

Zoey nodded. "Yes, I think so."

John motioned to the door. "Let's take the horses out of the barn. There could be aftershocks."

"What about Nanna Bell and Lily and Timothy?" Zoey asked as they led the horses out of the barn.

"I'm fine!" Timothy called. He met them outside of the barn with Sammy close at his heels.

"It's Lily and Nanna Bell I'm worried about," John explained as he led the horses into the small, fenced pasture beside the barn. "They went to the library."

Zoey pictured the library in an earthquake with books flying everywhere, but she shook her head and tried to think of something else. Then her mind went to aftershocks and how damaging they could be, but she shook her head again.

"Why do you keep shaking your head?" Timothy asked.

"I'm just trying to decide what to think about and what we should do now."

John looked at his phone, sighed, and put it back in his pocket. "I already tried to call Lily, but it seems the phone service isn't working. I want to go look for them, but I also don't want to leave you two."

"We'll be fine," Zoey said. "We'll stay outside here so that if there's an aftershock, we won't get hurt."

"Aftershocks are usually smaller, aren't they?" Timothy asked.

"Usually," John confirmed.

"Hello!" Lily's voice came ringing across the yard like a beautiful bell sounding good news. The others rushed to Lily and Nanna Bell, and they all rejoiced in being safely together.

"I'll go check on the chickens in their coop," Nanna Bell offered.

"Lily and I will check the house and see if we can smell any gas leaks," John said.

Zoey and Timothy found themselves alone.

"What were you doing when the earthquake hit?" Zoey asked Timothy.

"I was finishing my math lesson at the kitchen table when all of a sudden I felt a jolt, and then the whole world seemed to be rocking," Timothy said. "I quickly got under the table. It sounded like some dishes fell out

of the cupboards and broke, but I didn't look around much after it was over. I just dashed outside."

After explaining her experience with the earthquake, Zoey went with Timothy to inspect the outside of the barn. It looked fine except for the one broken window.

Just then, the ground started shaking again. The aftershock was very mild, just a slight rocking, but Zoey and Timothy still moved away from the barn out into the open.

"I think that was less than ten seconds," Timothy said when the rocking stopped.

"Oh, look!" Zoey pointed to the apple trees outside the pasture. "I think Dad forgot to latch the gate when we put the horses in the pasture. Look at the foal!"

Laughing, Zoey and Timothy walked over to the horses. The foal had grabbed onto a small branch of an apple tree and was shaking it around. White apple blossoms had fallen all over the foal's head and mane. She looked over at Zoey, so cute covered in the delicate white petals.

"Blossom! Oh, it's Blossom!" Zoey shouted so loudly that Timothy jumped.

"What do you mean?" Timothy asked, confused.

Zoey clapped her hands. "Blossom! That is what I'm going to call the foal!"

A few minutes later Lily, Nanna Bell, and

John rejoined the children.

"There is a cracked window and a lot of broken dishes in the kitchen," John reported. "Many things fell off shelves, but other than that it looks like everything is OK. I didn't smell a gas leak. I'm going to run down to Mrs. Bastian's house to see if she's OK."

He jogged off, and Nanna Bell said, "The chickens are fine."

Lily chimed in. "The power is out. We should collect flashlights, lanterns, and candles since the sun will be setting soon."

"With the power out, I'm glad it's a gentle, warm spring, so it's not really cold or hot," Zoey commented.

Lily nodded. "Agreed!"

"Do you think we'll have any more

aftershocks?" Timothy asked.

"Maybe," Lily said. "But they are likely to be much smaller, and the one we all just felt was tiny. Should we go in and start cleaning up?"

Everyone headed into the house. The work in the kitchen was slow because of all the broken glass. They worked carefully, and soon John joined them, confirming that all was well at Mrs. Bastian's house and that her assistant was helping her clean up.

"I dropped by Mrs. Minks's house too," John explained. "She and Jessica are OK. Their power is also out, but it looks like most of the city has power. Mrs. Minks was listening to her emergency radio. It seems the earthquake did not do any major damage."

"That's so great to hear," Lily said.

After the kitchen, they went room by room together, still able to see by the light of the sunset. In John and Lily's room, they were happy to see that although Lily's vase from the hidden room was knocked over on her dresser, it had not fallen off and was not even chipped.

Zoey picked up the vase and turned it around. "Hmmm. I still wonder what clue this vase holds."

Nanna Bell's clock from the hidden room was just fine too.

Zoey ran her hands around the wood of the clock. "I wonder how we will ever figure out the rest of the items. We've looked at this clock dozens of times and can't find any clues."

"I know," Timothy said. "Simon Roach

didn't make these mysteries easy, but they're fun!"

"Yes, they are fun!" Zoey agreed.

In Timothy's room, they found his painting from the hidden room on the floor. It had fallen off the wall.

Timothy picked it up gently and gasped. "Oh! The frame cracked in a couple of places. The wood was so old that I guess it's not a surprise. I wonder if we can fix it."

"What if we make a new frame?" John said. "I learned a bit about woodworking by building the chicken coop. With some help from the internet, I think we could do it."

"That would be great," Timothy responded.

"Let's look at the painting again," Zoey suggested, moving to stand by Timothy.

"Maybe we'll see something we missed before." Zoey scanned it intently. "You know," she pondered, "this scene looks a lot like the pictures we saw of the village Hirzel."

"The village from the map." Timothy nodded. "'lezrih' spelled backward."

"Yes," Zoey continued. "And the painting is signed by Hans Wolf. That is a German name, and the German dictionary we found in the library was signed by another person with the last name Wolf: Oma Wolf."

"Wait a minute!" Lily gasped. "You know I've started studying German pretty intensely. I just realized that Oma is not a name; it's a title. It means 'grandmother' in German!"

"Grandmother," Zoey echoed slowly. "Oh, this is exciting! There really is a mystery here, and so many connections. Your Johanna Spyri books are in German, Mom, and obviously the Wolfs are German. Johanna Spyri, the author of your books, was born in Hirzel, Switzerland, where they speak German, and Timothy's mysterious map is of Hirzel. Then there's this painting Timothy has . . . oh, I just know it is of Hirzel. Let's go to Hirzel and look for the house we see on this painting!"

John looked at Zoey with understanding eyes. "I'd love to go too, Zoey, but it really would be a shot in the dark. Even if we found the house, we'd have no idea what to do there."

Zoey nodded. "You're right. And I'm sure it would cost a lot for us all to travel to Switzerland. We'll find the clues somehow. I know it! Let's go check my room now."

The light outside was growing dim, but as they reached Zoey's room, one of the last bright rays of the peaceful sunset slanted through the window, shining a beam right on a pile of broken ceramic pieces on the floor. Zoey ran across the room and knelt down. Tears stung her eyes. "My ceramic oak tree! The earthquake knocked it off my shelf, and it shattered!"

CHAPTER 3

THROUGH THE TEARS THAT THREATENED
to spill from Zoey's eyes, she saw
something unexpected. In the middle of the
pile of broken pieces was a paper tightly rolled
and tied with an old piece of string. Zoey
wiped her eyes and gingerly picked it up.

"What is it?" Timothy whispered.

"I think it might be a clue," Nanna Bell
whispered, too, realizing that this was a special
moment for Zoey.

Zoey looked around at everyone. "Banana burrito humongous mosquito!" Zoey exclaimed. "The earthquake revealed the clue. It was inside the tree!"

She carefully slid the roll of paper out of the string and read the note aloud.

Go to my oak tree and put your back against August. Then go forward directly west for 20 feet and then directly south for 5 feet. Surely there you will find deep within the earth something that I hope you'll feel is of tremendous worth.

Sincerely,
Hannah

With wide eyes, Zoey looked up at the group that was now huddled around her. "Oh, I just can't believe it. There's a treasure buried near the tree. All we have to do is dig it up."

"But what does 'August' mean?" John asked.

Zoey read that part of the clue again: "Go to my oak tree and put your back against August."

Zoey stared at the message for a few moments. "I have no idea what 'August' means. How is a month at a tree?"

The room was quiet for a moment. Suddenly, Zoey jumped up so quickly that she startled the rest of the group. "Let's go to the tree and see if we can figure it out. Maybe if we look around the tree, we'll discover what 'August' means. Come on!" Zoey grabbed her jacket.

Lily laughed. "Hold on, Zoey! We can go, but it's starting to get dark, and we should use what little light there is left to inspect the rest of the house."

"We also need to put the horses back in the barn and feed the chickens," John noted.

"But then it will be dark," Zoey countered. "Can we still go to Hannah's white oak tree tonight? Oh please! We can bring lanterns and flashlights."

"It would be an adventure!" Nanna Bell pointed out.

"I really don't know how we can pass up a moonlight mystery!" agreed Lily as she smiled at John, who nodded his agreement.

"Oh thank you! Thank you!" Zoey gushed

as she hugged Nanna Bell and her parents.

A little while later, after taking care of all their responsibilities, the group set out for their adventure. Night had descended upon the farm. With no power in the house, the cloak of darkness seemed heavier than normal.

It's a little eerie being out here, Zoey thought as the group walked with a compass, shovels, and lanterns through the dark outlines of the whispering pine trees. No one spoke. The only sounds were the crunch of dirt beneath their feet and the steady chirping of crickets.

As the group entered the clearing, Hannah's white oak tree loomed before them, seeming to glow in the bright moonlight. As if on cue, an owl hooted as it swooped past them.

"Let's go see if we can find out what

'August' means!" The group followed Zoey's lead toward the tree.

Shining the lanterns all around, the group searched and searched. They ran their hands along all the parts of the tree they could reach. They searched around the base of the tree, and they held their lights up to inspect the thick lower branches. But they came across nothing except the big knob on the tree and the heart with "H+A" on it that they had already found.

Timothy spoke. "Maybe there are twelve notches on the tree, one for each month of the year, and the eighth one stands for August."

"Good idea," John said. "Let's look for twelve notches."

But twelve notches were not to be found.

Finally, Zoey gave up. "Well, we tried. I

wish that the Roach family would've made these clues just a little bit easier."

"We could just dig all around the tree and find it eventually," Timothy suggested.

"Yes, we could," John said. "That would be a ton of work. We should think about the clue for a while before we start digging. Maybe it will become more clear."

On the way back, Zoey sighed a few times.

"Disappointed?" Lily asked as she linked arms with Zoey.

"Yeah, a little," Zoey admitted. "I don't think we'll ever really know what 'August' means."

Lily nodded, and they walked a few more steps. "Is that all that's troubling you?" she asked, breaking the silence.

"I'm also thinking about volleyball," Zoey replied.

"Volleyball?" Lily asked in surprise.

Zoey explained Jessica's invitation to join her volleyball team. "Jessica says they really need me, but I'm nervous. I've never played a team sport before."

"Maybe it would be fun to try a team sport at least once," Lily counseled. "Sometimes it can be a good thing to try something new. But I support you one hundred percent either way. You should pray about it."

"Thank you, I will," Zoey said as she looked up into the dazzling night sky. "Do you really think that God, who created all those mighty stars, cares about something as small as my being on a volleyball team?"

"I don't think so; I know so," Lily assured her. "Are you worried and anxious about this decision?"

"Yes," Zoey answered.

"In the Bible, Peter taught us to cast all our anxieties upon God because He cares for us," Lily explained.

John added, "And not even a sparrow falls without His notice."

Nanna Bell chimed in. "He said He would wipe away every tear from your eye. Think of it; He knows every one of your tears."

Zoey laughed. "OK, I'm convinced that God cares about every little part of my life."

Her heart felt warm, and she knew it was true.

CHAPTER 4

A SWALLOW WAS MAKING A MUD NEST above Zoey's bedroom window, and the busy little bird was quite unaware that its scratching noises were disturbing Zoey's sleep. Bewildered, Zoey opened her eyes and noticed that her bedroom light was on. *That's strange*, she thought, noting that dawn was just arriving outside her window. In the back of her mind, she felt there was something significant about her light being on. Sitting up,

38

she stretched her arms into the air and looked
around. Her eyes stopped on her desk, and
her arms dropped. There on the desk lay the
note she had found in the broken ceramic oak
tree. It all came spinning back into her mind:
the earthquake, forgiving Misty Toes, naming
the foal, the note in the pile of broken ceramic

pieces, the hunt around the oak tree.

"Oh, the bedroom light," she said. "That means the power is back on."

After having a warm shower and throwing on clean clothes, Zoey knelt down by her bed and prayed. She talked to God about volleyball and how nervous she was to join the team. She also shared how it would allow her to try something new, get some exercise, and learn to work with a team. She felt a gentle peace.

After her prayer, Zoey went down to the kitchen for breakfast. Lily greeted her with a huge smile.

"Your birthday is tomorrow, Zoey! Dad and I have a special gift for you this year. I'll give you one clue: it's alive!"

Zoey was surprised. "Alive? Is it a cat?"

"I can't answer any questions," Lily said. "But I'm so excited that I can hardly keep it a secret. I'd better change the subject. Have you decided what to do about volleyball?"

"Yes. Can you text Jessica's mom and tell her that I want to join Jessica's volleyball team?"

"I sure will! When are practices?" Lily asked.

"Every Tuesday and Thursday night at seven o'clock. So I will practice tonight and Thursday if you can take me to practice. And then the first game is on Saturday morning. Will that work?"

Lily clapped her hands. "Yes! That works great! I'm excited for you."

After breakfast, Zoey thought that she and

Timothy should be allowed to start digging around the tree. "It's just so exciting. Can't we skip our schoolwork today?"

Nanna Bell and Lily shook their heads at the same time. "It is exciting, but it can wait until after your schoolwork."

A scowl stole across Zoey's face. "Fine," she snapped. "Let's get started, then." She went over and grabbed her math book and banged it onto the table. Even as she did, she knew it was wrong. Her emotions were just so strong.

Lily came over and sat next to her. "You're upset. I understand. Do you remember the things I taught you about—things you can do to get yourself out of an angry mood?"

Taking a deep breath and then letting it out slowly, Zoey mumbled in a low, unhappy voice,

"Pray in my heart, list off good things about my day, or force myself to smile."

"Well, which one do you want to choose?" Lily asked cheerfully.

"None of them," Zoey snapped.

"How about a smile?" Lily suggested. "Show me your biggest smile."

Zoey gave Lily the widest, fakest, cheesiest smile she could, and . . . it worked. She started to laugh, and she felt her anger quickly melt away.

School was actually fun. After math, they decided to replace their normal language arts with an in-depth study of Johanna Spyri and her books.

Lily brought out the basket she had taken to the library. It was full of books by Johanna

Spyri. They read the book titles and looked at the illustrations, which showed Swiss children and families in the Alps.

"I've started reading her books in English," Lily explained. "Her writing is beautiful."

Zoey researched and typed up a report on Johanna Spyri's life while Timothy wrote a report on the village of Hirzel. When she was finished, Zoey stood on a chair and read the report aloud to the family, including John, who took a break from preparing the campground for the groundbreaking ceremony.

After Zoey was done reading her report, she bowed and curtsied dramatically as her audience cheered and clapped wildly.

Zoey took a seat on the family room couch. "I wish I could go back in time and meet

Johanna Spyri
By Zoey

Johanna Heusser Spyri was born on June 12, 1827, in the Swiss village of Hirzel. She lived most of her life within just a few miles of her birthplace. Her first book was published in 1871 to help raise money for refugees of the Franco-Prussian War. She went on to write more than forty children's books in her lifetime, the most popular of which was *Heidi*. All of Johanna's charming books were based on her own life experiences, and her love of nature was obvious in her writing. She led a simple, quiet life until her death in 1901.

Johanna. There's not a lot written about her life. I have a million questions I would love to ask her."

"I wish I could go to Hirzel!" Timothy chimed in. "After researching the village, I think Zoey was on to something when she suggested we go there. There's even a museum in Hirzel about Johanna Spyri."

"I wish we could go too!" John agreed. "But it's extremely expensive. We need the money for the campground right now."

Timothy nodded. "I understand. I'll read my report now."

Afterward, Lily surprised everyone by announcing that she had gotten up quite early that morning to prepare a Swiss lunch: Älplermagronen, which seemed to Zoey like a

The Village of Hirzel
By Timothy

Not only is Hirzel, Switzerland, the village where Johanna Spyri grew up, but it is also famous for its beauty. Only about two thousand people live in this small piece of heaven. If you visited Hirzel, you could visit the Johanna Spyri Museum and see the actual books she read as a child, as well as some of the things from her home and many of her original books in German. You could also hike or ride bikes in the beautiful rolling hills, which are famous for having one lone linden tree on the top of several of the hilltops.

version of macaroni and cheese. It had macaroni noodles, cheese, potatoes, cream, and onions. And there was applesauce on the side.

Science and history were Swiss themed too.

To end the school day, Zoey and Timothy each chose a book by Johanna Spyri and did their personal reading out in the hammocks. At first, it was hard to concentrate because they were so excited to begin digging around Hannah's white oak tree, but the reading was so interesting that time went by quickly. Finally, the cousins were free to go dig. With gloves and shovels, they set out.

CHAPTER 5

"I SHOULD NOT HAVE DUG LIKE THAT FOR hours," Zoey moaned to Timothy as they walked home later that day. She rubbed her neck and shoulders. "I didn't think about having volleyball practice later, and we didn't even find anything."

"Yeah, practice may be hard for you tonight," Timothy agreed.

And they were both correct.

Zoey wasn't able to serve one ball over the

net, and every time a ball came to her, she either missed it or hit it out of bounds.

"Every single time!" Zoey told Lily that night. "It was terrible! But I did tell Coach Moody and the team that I had sore arms from digging on the farm. I told them I would be better prepared for practice on Thursday."

"So are you not going to dig around the oak tree at all until after Thursday?" Lily asked.

"I think I'd better wait until after the game on Saturday morning," Zoey sighed. "I don't want to let the team down."

"Good idea," Lily said. "For now, you should go soak your sore muscles in a hot bath and get some good sleep so you can enjoy your birthday tomorrow."

After a long, hot bath, Zoey gratefully curled

up in bed with the Johanna Spyri book she was reading, *Trini, the Little Strawberry Girl.*

The next morning, sunshine poured through the farm like liquid gold. Tall puffs of white clouds billowed in the sky. And the crab apple trees were ablaze with bright pink blossoms. It was as if the whole farm were celebrating Zoey's birthday.

Zoey and Timothy worked diligently on their chores and schoolwork until after lunch, when their work was interrupted by the sound of the doorbell.

"Oh! That must be your present," Lily bubbled, standing up. "All the way from Iceland."

"Iceland?" Zoey gasped.

"Yes, isn't it exciting? Now, you stay here,

and don't look out any of the windows," Lily directed.

The two cousins watched as Lily hurried to the door.

"What do you think it is?" Timothy asked.

Zoey shrugged. "I honestly have no idea. It's alive and from Iceland. Maybe some kind of Icelandic cat or rabbit?"

"But why get a cat or rabbit all the way from Iceland?" Timothy countered.

"That's true." Zoey was baffled.

They chatted for a few minutes about what the present might be and wondered why Lily was taking so long.

Finally, John, Lily, and Nanna Bell walked into the room with huge smiles.

Lily held up a scarf that she had folded into a

long strip. "I'm going to blindfold you, Zoey, and take you to your birthday gift!"

After blindfolding Zoey and leading her into the yard, Lily spun her around so that she had no idea which way she was going. Soon the smell of hay enveloped her, and she could tell she was in the barn. As the blindfold was taken off, Zoey gasped. There in front of her was the most beautiful horse she had ever seen. It was light cream in color with a very thick blonde mane.

"It's an Icelandic horse," John explained. "They are shorter than many other horses and are very gentle and calm. Ský is completely trained, and . . . well, I know you said you didn't want to ride a horse again, but we thought maybe if you had a gentle, well-trained

horse . . . you might want to ride her."

Zoey stood frozen in place. The barn was quiet. Everyone was staring at Zoey, waiting to see how she would respond.

"Ský is her name?" Zoey asked, without moving.

54

"Yes," Lily responded. "It means 'cloud' in Icelandic, but you can change her name if you'd like."

A single tear slid down Zoey's cheek. She stepped toward Ský and stroked her mane. "I don't want to change her name. I love her name. She is like a cloud. I'm amazed that you care so much about me that you brought Ský all the way from Iceland."

"We know that you once loved riding horses, and we hope you'll love it again," John explained.

"And with two horses," Lily continued, "you and I can ride together!"

"You talked about wanting to restore the horse arena on Badger Hills Farm," Nanna Bell added. "You were so excited about it."

Zoey nodded. "That's true." She thought for a moment. "I . . . think I can try riding Ský, but can I wait until after my volleyball game on Saturday? I don't want to risk getting hurt and not being able to go. They don't have enough people to play without me."

Lily walked over to Zoey and put her hand on her shoulder. "Zoey, it's not common for a person to get thrown off a gentle, trained horse. It really will be fine."

"I'd just like to be safe and wait until after the game on Saturday," Zoey maintained. "It's just a few days."

"Of course," Lily responded. "In the meantime, do you mind if I ride her a few times just to keep her ready for you?"

"Sure! I really like how you ride Misty Toes

almost every day. Thank you for doing that."

"My pleasure! She has been fine. I believe she is used to being ridden again," Lily said.

"I know," Zoey responded. "But I just can't bring myself to ride her. Even though I have forgiven her and love her, it just makes me feel panicked thinking about it."

Zoey glanced over atSký again, marveling at how beautiful and gentle she looked—just like a peaceful cloud.

Will I have enough courage to ride Ský? Am I just making excuses?

CHAPTER 6

S EEMS LIKE YOUR ARMS AREN'T FEELING any better today," Coach Moody said sharply as Zoey once again hit her serve into the net at Thursday night's practice.

Zoey felt her face getting red. To make matters worse, the coach's daughter, Madison, rolled her eyes at Zoey and shook her head.

The team started practicing receiving balls, and Zoey concentrated with all her might. To her relief, she hit several balls back over the net, and Jessica cheered for her. However, Zoey was painfully aware that she missed many more balls than she hit.

By the time practice was over, Zoey felt very discouraged and couldn't wait to get home. As they were leaving, Madison once again shook her head at Zoey.

I don't understand why she's not nice to me, Zoey thought. *After all, I'm just trying to help her team.*

The next day, Zoey found comfort in brushing and hugging the three beautiful horses—Ský, Blossom, and Misty Toes.

Timothy walked in. "How are the horses?"

"Great!" Zoey answered. "I love them so much. Horses have always helped me feel calm, and I need that right now. I'm so nervous about tomorrow's volleyball game. Everyone will be there watching! I don't want to ruin the team's chance of winning."

"It's really not about winning." Timothy took a stalk of celery out of his pocket and fed it to Blossom. "These city teams are meant for kids to learn and improve, and that's what you're doing. Who cares about winning? Just have fun."

Zoey sighed. "You're right, and I'm trying to have fun, but it's hard."

Timothy nodded. He could tell that Zoey was feeling sad and upset, so he changed the subject. "When will Blossom get trained for riding?"

"Not for a couple of years, but I think she is going to be a great riding horse," Zoey replied.

Timothy stroked Blossom's back and then turned to Zoey. "Hey, are you sure we can't go dig around Hannah's white oak tree? There's treasure there just waiting to be dug up! I can hardly wait."

"I know," Zoey agreed. "But I don't want sore arms. I need to be my best for the game tomorrow. Why don't I come watch you? I'll bring a blanket and lie under the tree and read while you dig."

Timothy laughed. "Oh sure! Make me do all the hard work, huh?"

They both laughed together as they left the barn.

To the cousins' disappointment, no treasure was found that day. The soil was hard and rocky, and the digging was hard for Timothy.

"I just wish we knew what 'August' meant," Zoey shared as they walked home. "Knowing that would help so much, but the instructions

on the note make no sense. What does it mean
to 'put your back against August'?"

Timothy shrugged. "It doesn't make sense
to me either."

That night, Zoey went to bed early so
that she was well rested for the game. The
next morning, she stretched, ate a healthy
breakfast, and even watched some volleyball
tips online to get prepared.

*I really don't want to let Jessica and the team
down*, she thought as she drove with her family
to the game.

Because there were barely enough players
for the team, there were no subs. Everyone had
to stay in the game the whole time.

Zoey focused and played better than she
had at any practice. Still, many of the balls that

she hit went out of bounds, and some balls she missed altogether. In the last set, Coach Moody called for a time-out.

"The score is tied," she said. "We're not going to win if any of the balls go to Zoey. She can't seem to hit anything, and we're going to lose the game because of her." The coach turned to her daughter. "Madison, anytime a ball is coming toward Zoey, you get it. I don't care how close it is to Zoey. It's your ball. You get it!"

Zoey's heart dropped. She glanced over at Jessica and saw that her friend was furious.

"But, Coach, that's not–" Jessica began, but the buzzer went off. Time-out was over, and everyone was running back onto the court.

Zoey couldn't believe the coach had been

so unkind. Her eyes burned with tears, but she held them back. *With all my heart, I just want this game to be over,* Zoey thought. She considered running out of the gym but forced herself to stay.

Never had Zoey felt so embarrassed as those last fifteen minutes of the game. Madison continually jumped in front of Zoey and hit the ball. Even when the ball was coming straight for Zoey, Madison ran to the ball and took it. And every time, the ball went smoothly where Madison wanted it to go.

From the sidelines, Zoey heard the coach call, "That's it, Madison. Keep it up!"

The team won, but Zoey didn't feel like celebrating. After grabbing her water bottle, she ran out of the gym, the tears now flowing freely as she stood by the car, waiting for the rest of her family.

"What happened, Zoey?" Lily asked as she approached the car.

Zoey told her family everything the coach had said. She had never seen John look so angry. "I wondered why that girl kept taking all of your balls. I can't believe a coach would tell someone to do that. It's such poor sportsmanship. Winning is not nearly as important as playing kindly and showing good sportsmanship."

Across the parking lot, Zoey could see Madison and Coach Moody walking toward their car. Madison saw Zoey and made a crying motion, putting her hands into fists and moving them back and forth over her eyes.

Zoey jumped into the car and slammed the door.

Back at home, John and Lily sat with Zoey for a long time as she lay in bed for a nap.

"You don't have to stay on the team," Lily said. "No one should be treated like that by anyone, especially a coach. A coach should be someone who builds people up and cares more about the people playing than about winning a game."

"I can talk to your coach," John said.

Zoey sniffed. "I'll think about what to do."

After John and Lily left, Zoey stared out her window until she fell asleep.

Unfortunately, she didn't feel any better after the short nap. She tried a forced smile, but it didn't work very well this time.

I guess a forced smile can work for small things, but maybe not big things, Zoey thought.

Later, Zoey made her way out to the stable. After the volleyball game, she didn't feel excited about riding, but she also didn't want to disappoint Lily. Zoey stood beside Ský as Lily held the reins. It was time to ride. Zoey put her hand on the saddle and put her foot in the stirrup, ready to mount the horse. Ský took a slight step forward, and panic welled up in Zoey. She took her foot off the stirrup and stepped away from the horse.

"It's OK, Zoey. I have a tight hold on the reins," Lily said.

Zoey hung her head. "I . . . I don't know how to explain it, but something happened to me when Misty Toes threw me off. My heart is beating so fast, and I feel like I'm drowning. I just . . . can't!"

She ran out of the barn, tears streaming again.

CHAPTER 7

THE NEXT DAY, ZOEY COULDN'T SEEM TO shake her gloomy mood and the feeling that everything was going wrong in her life. Even the message and music at church did little to lift her mood.

Monday was no better. After getting all of her schoolwork finished, Zoey lay in her bed all afternoon. At dinner, she was quiet and withdrawn, and everyone was worried about her. Zoey felt bad about being so grumpy, and that made her feel even more gloomy.

Very early on Tuesday morning, the swallows woke Zoey up again. She rolled over, and her arm hit something hard and crinkly on her bed. Sitting up, Zoey found a package lying on her bed. It was wrapped in white paper and tied with a big purple bow. A note attached to the top read "My publisher sent this proof to review before the final print run. Let me know what you think! B.B."

She untied the ribbon and tore the paper off the package. A beautiful book titled *The Mystery Writer* lay in her hands. She turned the book over and read the back cover.

"Wait," Zoey said. "Is this—? It is!" She hugged the book to her chest. It was the book Mrs. Bastian had written about Zoey.

Holding the book in her hands, Zoey thought about the thank-you cards her mother had created and the experience that had inspired Mrs. Bastian to write the book Zoey now held in her hands.

Zoey went to her desk and searched through a drawer until she found the note her mother had left in the chest on top of all of the thank-you cards.

Sitting at her desk, Zoey read the note.

My Dearest Zoey,

I have no money to give, but I have chosen to leave you a gift of great value. For years I have painted thank-you cards by hand—one thousand of them. The gift of gratitude will help you almost more than anything, especially when you are facing your greatest trials. It's now up to you to find one thousand people to thank with these cards.

My love always,

Mom

Zoey searched the drawer again for the news article Lily had printed out for her. With misty eyes, she read the news article.

Over the past several months, someone has been busy writing and anonymously delivering hundreds of thank-you cards to citizens of our community. Each card appears to be hand painted with a different painting, and the cards are simply signed as being from "Your Friend." Stories have been pouring into the news station about these cards and the impact they are having. One man who was homeless explained, "When I received a note thanking me for always waving to people and making them happy, something changed in me. I realized that my life had purpose, and there was hope for my future, so I got a job at the pet shelter."

If you were one of the people blessed to receive one of these cards and would like to share it, we will be publishing some of the cards in a new weekly column titled "Thank-You Card Mystery."

Zoey ran and jumped back on her bed. A smile crept onto her face as she recalled meeting Mrs. Bastian. Zoey had felt such shock when the famous author told her that she wanted to write a story about her experience, starting with her life on the ranch in Canada and covering her mother's death, her move to the city, the mystery of her mother's trunk, and then the thousand thank-you notes that Zoey and Timothy wrote and delivered anonymously all over the city.

Zoey opened the book and began reading. All morning she read, laughing and crying.

Lily peeked in and, a few minutes later, brought a tray of breakfast to Zoey.

Zoey kept reading, feeling her whole perspective about life change again, as it had months ago when she wrote the one thousand thank-you notes with Timothy. She started to feel more grateful and less gloomy.

Later, Lily quietly brought in a tray with lunch, which Zoey absently nibbled as she read.

Finally, Zoey read the last page, closed the book with a smile, and looked over at the clock.

"Five thirty!" Zoey jumped out of bed, quickly showered and dressed and then knelt beside her bed to pray. Afterward, she rushed down the stairs and burst into the family room.

"I need thank-you notes!" Zoey said. "Can we go to the store?"

"Just a moment," Nanna Bell said, a twinkle in her eye. She disappeared into the kitchen and returned with a shopping bag. "I thought some thank-you notes might be needed, so I went to the store this morning."

Zoey rushed to Nanna Bell and hugged her. "You're so thoughtful! Thank you."

"You're welcome," Nanna Bell replied.

Zoey turned to Lily. "I've realized that a forced smile helps me get out of little bad moods, but when I have a big bad mood, I need to do something bigger to get out of it, something for other people. It's time to write more thank-you notes."

"That's a great idea," Lily said. "But first, let's get some dinner and get you to volleyball practice."

CHAPTER 8

T HE NEXT AFTERNOON, NINE THANK-YOU notes sat stacked on the table next to Zoey. They were for Mrs. Bastian; Nanna Rose and Papa George; the mail carrier; Mrs. Minks; Mrs. Sanchez, Timothy's art teacher and their family friend; the elderly man who ran the bakery down the street; the woman who taught Zoey's youth class at church; the doctor who had put staples in her head; and Mr. Garcia, the stamp and art collector.

To give her hand a break, Zoey helped John feed the chickens. Then she sat back down at the kitchen table and wrote one more note.

Dear Coach Moody,
 I wanted to thank you for coaching our team. I know it's a volunteer position, and it takes a lot of your time and effort.
 I also wanted to let you know that my feelings were very hurt at the last game. I have never played a team sport before. It took a lot of courage for me to join the team and push myself to do something new. I don't feel that winning is as important as teaching kindness, teamwork, and good sportsmanship. Could we give each other a new start?
 Sincerely,
 Zoey

At five o'clock, Lily drove Zoey to Coach Moody's house, and Zoey gave the note to the teenage boy who opened the door.

As Zoey got back in the car, Lily smiled. "I'm so proud of you. Oh, and I just got a text message from Mrs. Minks. Jessica and Diego want to bring the volleyball net over to practice serving with you. What do you think?"

"Sure!" Zoey agreed, grateful that the gloomy mood had fled away.

For two hours, Zoey, Timothy, Jessica, and Diego worked on serving in the backyard where they set up the net. Finally, most of Zoey's serves were making it over the net. Everyone cheered her on, and she started to think that volleyball was actually pretty fun.

"Can we practice again tomorrow afternoon

before the team practice?" Zoey asked.

"Sure!" Jessica smiled. "I'll leave my net here and be over at four o'clock tomorrow."

The sun was setting, and the world was full of splendid light. Humming, Zoey went into the barn to care for the horses. As she was finishing up, Nanna Bell joined her.

"I have an idea," Nanna Bell began slowly. "I pray about you every day, asking God if there is anything I can do to help you. I believe that God gave me an idea."

Zoey was interested. "What is it?"

"Well, I was thinking about this barn and how it was built step-by-step. First, the foundation was poured, then the frame was put up, and so on. How would you feel about taking little steps toward riding Ský? For example, the first thing you could do is just put your foot in the stirrup and stand yourself up in it, but not get on the horse. Then eventually, you can swing your leg over the horse and sit on her but get off immediately. You can do that over and over until you're ready for the next step."

Zoey tapped her chin as she thought about Nanna Bell's idea, and then she gave a nod. "I think that's brilliant. I want to start right now!"

Nanna Bell and Zoey saddled up Ský. Then, with her heart beating fast, Zoey put her foot in the stirrup, grabbed the pommel on the saddle, and stood up in the stirrup. She got right off and then laughed.

"That was not bad at all!"

She did it again and again. Her heart no

longer beat quickly. She felt no panic.

"Oh, Nanna Bell," Zoey gushed as she hugged her grandmother, "I'm so grateful for you. This might actually work. Thank you! Can we keep this just between you and me right now?"

Nanna Bell smiled knowingly. "I think that's a good idea. It might make you feel less pressured."

Hand in hand, Nanna Bell and Zoey walked toward the house as dusk descended on the farm and deep shadows gathered under the trees.

What a long, exhausting, hard, great, wonderful, unexpected day, Zoey thought.

CHAPTER 9

A CRACK OF THUNDER HERALDED THE start of rain the next afternoon. Zoey, Timothy, and Nanna Bell left their schoolwork at the family room table and went to the window to watch the storm.

Sheets of rain blew nearly sideways, and the driving wind wildly swayed the branches of the trees.

"This is quite the storm!" Timothy declared after several minutes.

"I guess I won't be practicing volleyball today." Zoey frowned. "Look at how much rain is coming down."

"Let's get the fireplace going and make some hot chocolate," Nanna Bell suggested.

The kids cheered, and soon the small group was sitting by the glowing fire, sipping hot chocolate and waiting for Nanna Bell to start an art lesson.

She took her tablet out and pulled up a painting. "We've been talking about trees in botany for science, so I wanted to show you some beautiful paintings I found of some trees. They are by August Cappelen, who was a Norwegian painter."

Timothy sat up straight. "Wait! What was that name again?"

"August Cappelen," repeated Nanna Bell.

"August!" Timothy exclaimed. "I didn't know that could be a first name. I've been thinking so much about the oak tree mystery, and I've started wondering if the heart with 'H+A' has anything to do with it. Could the 'A' in the heart stand for the name August?"

Zoey shot up from the couch and pressed her hands together. "Oh! Maybe so!"

Nanna Bell stood up too. "This is exciting! I have an idea. You know that I love researching my ancestors. I subscribe to websites online where I can search for information about people from times past. What if we search for Hannah Roach and see if we can discover who she married?"

"Excellent idea!" Zoey exclaimed.

"Wahoo! Wahoo! Wahoo!" Timothy cheered.

Sammy started barking, and Lily and John came into the room.

"What is this noise all about?" Lily said. She grinned at the children.

"August!" shouted Zoey and Timothy at the same time. They fell onto the couch in a laughing fit as Sammy continued to bark.

John gave a crooked smile and shook his head at the children. "What is going on?"

Nanna Bell explained, and then they all huddled around her at the computer while she searched.

"Here's Hannah's birth record," Nanna Bell said after a couple of minutes. "Her father was Simon Roach, and her mother was

Tabitha Wolf."

"What?" Zoey blurted. She whipped her head toward Timothy.

"Wolf!" they said at the same time.

"Wait a minute," John said. "Wasn't the dictionary from someone with the last name Wolf?"

"Yes!" Zoey cried. "It was from Oma Wolf, which we know from Mom's German studies means 'grandmother.'"

"Grandmother," Nanna Bell repeated. "Let me see if I can find Hannah's grandmother on this website."

As Nanna Bell clicked away on the computer, the rest of the group looked on eagerly, feeling loose threads of the mystery starting to come together at last.

"Here it is!" Nanna Bell said. "Hannah's grandparents were Karl and Astrid Wolf, who lived in Switzerland."

"That means the German dictionary was from Hannah's grandmother!" Zoey exclaimed.

Timothy had been scanning the computer screen. "Oh! Hey, look, everyone! It looks like Karl and Astrid Wolf had two children, Tabitha and Hans. Remember the name on the painting I got from the hidden room? Hold on. I'll go get it!"

Timothy zoomed out of the room and returned soon with his painting. Out of breath, he said, "Look! In the bottom right-hand corner, the painting is signed by Hans Wolf!"

"So much is coming together," Lily said. "This is exciting!"

Nanna Bell started tapping again on the keyboard. "It looks like Tabitha immigrated to the United States when she was twenty years old, but her parents and her brother stayed in Switzerland. It seems they died there. Tabitha married Simon Roach when she was twenty-two years old."

"So, let's go back a little bit. Is there anything about who Hannah married?" Zoey asked.

Nanna Bell searched the records for a moment and then smiled. "Why yes, it says here that she married a man named August."

"Banana burrito humongous mosquito! The initials H+A must be for Hannah and August."

Zoey exclaimed. "I'm going to grab the note that was hidden in my ceramic oak tree."

She dashed out of the room. When she returned with the note, she unrolled it and read aloud.

Go to my oak tree and put your back against August. Then go forward directly west for 20 feet and then directly south for 5 feet. Surely there you will find deep within the earth something that I hope you'll feel is of tremendous worth.

Sincerely,
Hannah

Zoey's eyes were shining. "It makes sense now. I just need to put my back against the carved heart and go directly west for twenty feet and then directly south for five feet and then dig!" She jumped up. "Let's go!"

In response, a rumble of thunder echoed through the farm. Zoey looked over at the windows, which were streaming with little rivers of rain.

"I think you're going to have to wait," Lily said reluctantly. "All this rain and mud would make digging quite difficult."

Zoey flopped onto the couch. "You're right."

CHAPTER 10

As SHE WALKED INTO THE GYM, ZOEY felt nervous. She hadn't seen Coach Moody since she had dropped off the thank-you note. *I hope she will be kinder,* thought Zoey. *Maybe she'll even apologize.*

The coach, however, did not apologize. Throughout practice, she glared at Zoey and shook her head with a frown the few times that Zoey missed a ball.

I've improved a lot, and I'm hitting most

94

balls correctly. And she is not saying anything about it, Zoey thought. *I wonder if she did not get my note.*

But Madison soon put that question to rest when she walked by and said with a snicker, "Nice note."

Halfway through practice, a tall girl with long black braids came into the gym and onto the court.

"This is Jane," the coach told everyone. "She hasn't played much volleyball, but she is the star basketball player at the middle school. I practiced with her all week, and she's already picking up volleyball much better than some other people have."

Zoey's face felt hot. She was sure the coach was talking about her.

"We have one more game. If we win, we take the championship. Let's finish practice with Jane, and then I'll see you all on Saturday morning for the game."

The next morning, the sun seemed to be taking a nap in a gray blanket of clouds, but by lunchtime, the blue sky sparkled. Zoey had gone to her Friday homeschool group that morning, and she was so excited that they were now home. Today was the groundbreaking ceremony for the campground. The mayor was there, along with other important people from the city. They were excited about the campground and the great benefit it would be to the city.

Zoey smiled as John and Lily together stuck their shovels into the dirt while everyone

cheered. The tractors that had been waiting roared to life and began lifting their big scoops. Building the campground had begun!

It wasn't until a couple of hours later that everyone was back home, and the whole family was ready to go to Hannah's white oak tree.

As they walked through the little forest, the

ground was dappled by golden sunlight that found its way through the leaves. The cool stream laughed softly, and the bees droned. All around them, the air was sweet with the smell of wild lilacs.

Coming out of the trees, Zoey could see Hannah's white oak tree in the distance. The tree with its thick, twisted branches was so beautiful that Zoey got goosebumps.

Zoey and Timothy broke into a run and reached the tree out of breath. Quickly, they found the carved heart, and Zoey ran her fingers across the letter "A."

As soon as the rest of the group arrived at the tree, Zoey put her back to the heart, took the note from her pocket, and read it aloud one last time.

Go to my oak tree and put your back against August. Then go forward directly west for 20 feet and then directly south for 5 feet. Surely there you will find deep within the earth something that I hope you'll feel is of tremendous worth.

Sincerely,
Hannah

John handed Timothy the tape measure. "I guess this is it. We are about to find something of great worth deep within the earth. I'll hold the compass so I can go directly west while you measure."

Timothy nodded. Nearly trembling with

excitement, he measured twenty feet directly west and John marked the spot with a big rock. Zoey walked to the rock, and John handed the compass to Lily. "You should finish!"

Taking his father's example of thoughtfulness, Timothy gave the tape measure to Nanna Bell. "You should measure this time. We should all take part in solving this mystery!"

"Thank you, Timothy. That's very kind of you," Nanna Bell responded.

Working with both the compass and the tape measure, Lily and Nanna Bell carefully measured five feet directly south of the first rock. They placed another rock on that spot, and Zoey walked to it.

With her foot, Lily made a medium-sized

circle around the rock. "Hopefully we measured carefully enough that the item will be within this circle."

Two people at a time worked with the shovels, everyone taking turns. The ground was still a little wet from yesterday's storm, but it was dry and compact under the top layer.

"How deep do you think it will be?" Timothy asked Zoey as John and Lily were digging.

"It's hard to tell," John replied. "It seems to be fairly deep."

As the sun set low behind the trees, the group continued to dig. Zoey started to lose hope that they would ever find the treasure. The ground was hard and rocky, so it was hard to dig fast. They had dug down three feet already and found nothing. She had

been so sure they would find something that, until now, she hadn't even considered the possibility that there might be nothing there.

Wiping his brow, John finished his turn and handed his shovel to Zoey.

Determined to find the item before the sun set, Zoey quickly plunged the shovel into the hole and was shocked when the shovel hit something completely solid. There was a funny sound like metal hitting metal.

Everyone froze.

"We've found it," Zoey whispered.

CHAPTER 11

T HE GROUP BURST FROM THEIR SHOCKED silence into a flurry of movement. All of them dropped to their knees and began wildly scooping dirt from around the object.

It soon became apparent that the item was rectangular and made of metal.

The ground was hard, and scooping the dirt with their hands wasn't working well, so Timothy found a rock and started scraping the dirt from around the item. Everyone else

followed his idea, and soon the item in the ground took shape as the dirt around it was removed.

"It's a metal box!" Zoey declared.

"It's a big metal box," Nanna Bell noted.

John and Lily finally lifted the heavy box out of the hole and set it gently on the dirt. It was the size of a very large picnic basket.

"It's rusted and looks so old," Timothy noted.

"It is old. It was probably put there in the 1890s, which was about one hundred thirty years ago," Nanna Bell replied.

"Wow," Zoey said as she looked down at the box. "I can't even imagine what's in there."

"I don't think we can carry this home. It's too heavy," John said, looking up at the fiery sunset that spread above them. "I'll run home and get a wheelbarrow to put it in."

Half an hour later, they finally had the box home. They brushed the dirt off and set it on a table in the family room. The early spring air had turned cold, so Nanna Bell started a fire in the fireplace.

"Well, Zoey," Lily said with a smile, "you should be the one to open it."

Zoey stepped toward the box and placed her hand on the cold metal. There was no lock, so it opened easily, but the hinges creaked loudly. Zoey peered into the box.

"It's another metal box," she said.

With Timothy's help, Zoey lifted out the second metal box. It, too, was rusted and old. Zoey couldn't believe what they found inside.

108

Timothy chuckled. "It's another metal box."

The third box was the size of a large book.

"There's no way another box is in this one," Zoey declared.

Everyone gathered more closely around Zoey. All was quiet except for the crackling of the fire. Slowly, Zoey opened the lid to find a variety of objects lying inside.

First, she lifted out a piece of polished wood. "Oh!" Zoey caught her breath. "It's another piece of the Nativity set!"

Timothy smiled. "It's an angel!"

Zoey handed the angel to Nanna Bell. "Here! You can add this to your Nativity set."

Next, Zoey picked up a very old baseball card with worn edges. "Did Hannah like baseball?" Zoey wondered.

"That is so cool!" Timothy burst out. "A

ROGER·A·COOK
CENTER FIELD - CLEVELAND

baseball card from before the year 1900."

Zoey handed it to Timothy. "I want you to have it."

"Really? Oh, thank you!" Timothy gushed.

Turning her attention back to the box,
Zoey gently lifted out an old brass button. "It
must be a button that belonged to Hannah,"
Zoey marveled in a
quiet tone. "Look
at the flower on the
button. Oh, it's
just so neat to be
holding a button
that Hannah once

held. I know she's not my ancestor, but I feel
close to her. I want to know more about her."

"Maybe those letters will tell you more." Lily
pointed to a small bundle of letters, the last
items in the box.

Carefully, Zoey picked up the letters. The
worn string the letters were tied in fell apart

and gently slipped off the bundle. Four pieces of paper were folded in half. The papers were so brittle that when Zoey unfolded the first paper, it broke in half. She gasped.

"It's OK," Nanna Bell assured Zoey. "You should still be able to read it."

Quickly, Zoey scanned the handwritten text. She then looked up, her eyes sparkling.

"This letter mentions Hannah's pets and the animals on the farm. She even had a horse! I can't wait to read this whole letter later," Zoey gushed.

The next two letters were also full of information about Hannah and her life. But the last letter was different. It was short, and its message caught everyone off guard.

Clue: The love on the vase will show you the place.

"You're kidding!" John said. "Another clue already? Lily, you should go get the vase you chose from the hidden room!"

Lily disappeared and returned quickly, cradling the vase in her hands. "Can you read the clue again?" she asked Zoey.

"The love on the vase will show you the place," Zoey read slowly.

Nanna Bell got the magnifying glass and handed it to Lily. For a few minutes, Lily studied the vase. Then she shook her head. "I just don't get it. The clue makes no sense."

"Can I look at it?" Zoey asked.

"Sure! But be very careful," Lily said as she passed the vase to Zoey.

Sitting on the couch, Zoey used the magnifying glass to study every inch of the vase. Her mind was making connections fast.

"I figured it out," she whispered at last.

"You did?" Lily responded.

"Yes. What symbol represents love?"

"A heart," Timothy declared.

"That's right!" Zoey nodded. "And there is a heart on this vase. It's very small, but it's definitely a heart. And guess where it is?"

"Where?" the rest of the group said at the same time.

A smile slowly spread on Zoey's face. She stood up and walked over to the crackling fire. After putting her hands on the brick fireplace, she looked up to where the chimney met the ceiling.

"There's a little cottage on the vase that has a brick chimney. One of the bricks at the top of the chimney has a heart on it—a very clear, cute little heart, the symbol of love. The clue says, 'The love on the vase will show you the place.' The place is the chimney."

The room was still until John finally broke the silence. "So . . . you think that means that the place we are supposed to look is . . . in the chimney of this house?"

Zoey nodded. "Exactly!"

CHAPTER 12

TIMOTHY RAN TO THE COAT RACK, grabbed his coat, and started putting it on. "Come on! Let's go!"

"Where?" John asked in confusion.

"The chimney, of course!" Timothy called out as he moved toward the front door.

"We can't get to the chimney right now," John replied. "It's dark."

Timothy stopped walking and sighed. "Oh, right. I was so excited that I forgot what time it is. But we can go up there in the morning."

Zoey smiled at how excited Timothy was.

Lily chimed in. "We can't do it in the morning. Zoey has her final championship volleyball game, and we are all really excited about going."

"Not only that," John added, "but we don't have the right equipment to get up on the roof. We need a ladder that is tall enough, and we need to find out how to get up there safely. And when I say 'we,' I actually mean 'me' because I am not letting you children up on this steep roof. I also have no idea how to take a chimney apart, and, to be honest, it feels a little crazy. Are we really going to disassemble our chimney looking for something that Simon Roach might have left there?"

"Yes!" everyone said at the same time.

John laughed. "You're right! After all, Simon Roach left us a stamp worth over a million dollars! Who knows what could be in the chimney?"

With excitement and a sense of adventure whirling around them, Zoey and her family ate a late dinner in front of the crackling fireplace. Along with imagining what might be in the chimney, they talked about the items for which clues had not yet been found: Timothy's painting and map, Nanna Bell's clock, Lily's books, and John's photo album of the Roach family.

After cleaning up dinner, the family gathered on the family-room couches for a short Bible study. They had been studying the

Sermon on the Mount in Matthew, chapters five through seven, taking turns reading verses and discussing them.

When it was Zoey's turn, she read aloud, "Lay not up for yourselves treasures upon earth, where moth and rust doth corrupt, and where thieves break through and steal: But lay up for yourselves treasures in heaven, where neither moth nor rust doth corrupt, and where thieves do not break through nor steal: For where your treasure is, there will your heart be also."

The room was still and peaceful as everyone reflected on that important verse and its words about treasure.

Zoey had snuggled up to Lily, and she felt Lily's arm wrapped lovingly around her as they sat on the couch.

"Treasure," John said quietly. "It's very exciting to think of a possible treasure in the chimney, but my greatest treasures are here, and there, and there, and there, and there." John had pointed to the Bible and then to each member of the family around him in the room.

Zoey's heart felt as if it would burst. A little prayer slipped out of her heart and soared toward heaven. *Thank You, God, for giving me this family after my mom died. Thank You for giving me people to love and who love me.*

⟋⟍

The next morning, everyone excitedly piled into the car to go support Zoey at her volleyball game.

"I'm glad I chose to continue volleyball.

I really like it," Zoey said to her family as they drove. She thought about earlier that morning, when Timothy had gone outside with her to practice. Zoey had hit the ball correctly most of the time. She felt quite confident that she could contribute to the team today.

With the addition of Jane to the team, they had an extra person. That meant the coach could rotate players and give one person the chance to rest. Zoey's heart sank when she realized she was the first person that Coach Moody had chosen to sit out.

But Zoey chose to smile and cheer on her team. She noted that Jane, being new to the sport, was really good, but she did sometimes miss balls.

Fifteen minutes into the game, Zoey looked around, confused. Coach Moody still hadn't rotated her in.

When the game was half over and the team had a break, Zoey finally worked up enough courage to go over and talk to the coach.

"Ummm, Coach Moody, I was wondering when you are going to rotate me in," Zoey said.

"It's not required that I rotate you in," the coach stated simply.

"But . . . I'm one of the team members," Zoey insisted kindly. "And I've improved a lot. I'd really like a chance to play."

With a frown, Coach Moody said, "This is the final championship game. We want to win." And with that Coach Moody turned her back to Zoey and began talking to her daughter, Madison, who gave Zoey an unkind look.

Zoey bit her lip and went to sit back down. It took everything inside her to keep sitting on that bench.

The team was halfway through the last set, and a time-out had been called. As the coach was giving instructions, Jessica interrupted the coach. "Sorry to interrupt, Coach Moody, but why are you not letting Zoey play?"

"I have my reasons. Don't worry about it," the coach responded. "Now listen up, everyone. Let's get out there and win!"

Jessica folded her arms. "It's unfair, and it's not kind that you're not letting Zoey play. I'm not playing if Zoey doesn't get to come in."

124

Another girl folded her arms too. "I'm not playing either."

One by one, each of the other girls on the team did the same thing, except for Madison.

The whistle blew, and the girls with folded arms didn't move.

"Come on!" the referee called. "You have to get on the court now, or you will be penalized."

The girls still didn't move.

The referee blew his whistle and called a penalty on the team. "Do you want another penalty?" he asked. "Get on the court!"

When the girls still refused to move, Timothy started chanting from the bleachers, "Zoey! Zoey!"

Soon the whole audience was standing and

chanting Zoey's name. Their voices thundered in the gym, and Zoey could see that some of the girls, including Jessica, had tears on their cheeks.

They are doing what is right, Zoey thought, *and they can feel it.*

"Fine!" the coach snapped. "Zoey can play."

As Zoey walked onto the court, the crowd broke into wild applause.

Trembling, Zoey stood on the court, not sure she could hit the ball if it came to her. Everything was whirling in her mind, and she was worried about letting everyone down.

The first ball came directly to her. She hit it, but it went out of bounds.

Still, the crowd cheered with phrases such as "It's OK!" and "You can do it!"

Madison walked by Zoey and hissed, "You're going to make us lose!"

A couple of minutes later, Zoey hit the ball, and this time it was a beautiful spike that won the team a point. Once again, the crowd broke into wild applause.

The next time the ball came to Zoey, she got another point. But the time after that, she missed the ball entirely.

Finally, Zoey's team was at match point. If they won the next point, they would win the game and the championship.

The other team served. Time seemed to stand still as the ball sliced through the air, coming directly toward Jessica. The room was holding its breath. Jessica bumped the ball, the setter did a beautiful set right toward Zoey, and Zoey spiked the ball right where no one was standing on the other side. The ball hit the ground, and Zoey's team won the game!

The team was cheering. The crowd was cheering. Zoey looked over at Coach Moody, and she stood with folded arms and a scowl. Zoey realized sadly, *She's so angry about my playing that she is not even happy about winning, and winning meant so much to her.*

Several minutes later all the players had medals placed around their necks. Zoey loved the feel of the satin ribbon and the weight of the medal. She examined the medal and thought it was beautiful.

Outside, Zoey's family chatted excitedly as they walked toward the car. Suddenly, barking and screaming made them all turn around.

A dog was loose and chasing Madison across the grass. Madison was screaming. The dog's owner caught hold of its leash just as it jumped at Madison. She was pushed forward into a huge mud puddle and fell flat on her face.

As Madison stood up, everyone, including Coach Moody and Zoey, gathered around her. Someone offered Madison a towel, and she began to wipe away what mud she could. Then she saw her medal. It was dented—probably from hitting a rock that was in the puddle— and the beautiful ribbon was covered in mud. Madison tried wiping the mud off the ribbon with the towel, but everyone could see that it was stained.

"My medal is ruined!" Madison huffed. She turned toward the dog's owner. "This is all your fault! Look at my ruined medal!"

Zoey looked down at her medal and then back at Madison. She hesitated a moment but then stepped forward and took off her medal. "Here," she said to Madison. "You should take mine. After all, you are the best player on the team. You really deserve it. Besides, I was only here for two games, and you were here for the whole season."

Madison looked at Zoey in stunned silence and then slowly reached out her hand and took the medal. "Thank you," she said meekly.

CHAPTER 13

PILES OF WHITE CLOUDS DRIFTED SLOWLY in the sky above the barn. Zoey's family had eaten lunch after the game, and then Zoey announced that she had quite a big surprise to show them.

"Nanna Bell is getting it ready," she said to Timothy, John, and Lily. "Come outside with me!"

As they stepped out onto the porch, they were surprised to see an unfamiliar, shiny blue car pulling into their driveway. ... even more surprised when Coach Moody and Madison got out of the blue car. Both looked uncomfortable as they walked toward Zoey.

Coach Moody held a white box out toward Zoey. "French butter cookies from our favorite bakery. It's my way of saying I'm sorry and thank you. Thank you for being an example to us. You're right. Winning doesn't matter nearly as much as kindness. You showed us that, and we won't forget it, will we, Madison?"

Madison looked at the ground, drawing a circle with her toe. "Um, no, I guess we won't."

Without another word, Coach Moody and Madison got back in their car and left.

"Wow," Zoey said, "I wasn't expecting that

...ne white box and

...e a cookie. After biting into

...ie herself, she motioned to the others.

"Come on! Follow me to the barn."

When they got to the barn, they were surprised to see Nanna Bell holding Misty Toes's reins. She led the horse to Lily.

"Here, take Misty Toes. Someone wants to go on a horseback ride with you," Nanna Bell explained.

"Someone? What do you mean? Who wants to ride with me?" Lily asked as she took the reins.

Nanna Bell then opened a stall and took out Ský, who was fully saddled and ready to ride. With a wink and a smile, Nanna Bell handed the reins to Zoey.

"I do!" Zoey said.

Everyone then watched with breathless excitement as Zoey mounted Ský. "Come on, Lily! Let's go for a ride!" she called as she started toward the barn door.

Mother and daughter rode their horses slowly down a trail that wound through the farm. Zoey explained how she had taken small steps every day to get to the point that she could ride Ský.

"Wow!" Lily said with a shake of her head. "You are quite an amazing girl. I am proud of you for winning your championship game, and a thousand times more proud of you for showing kindness. What you did for Madison today—giving her your medal—was an incredible act of charity. And now I see that you have worked hard to overcome your fear of riding. How does it feel to be on a horse again?"

"Amazing!" Zoey sang.

She tilted her head back and watched a flock of geese honking in the sky. She then breathed in deeply. Every little breeze that fanned her face carried the scent of flowers.

"Amazing!" Zoey whispered again.

Continue the adventures of Timothy and Zoey with *Clue in the Chimney*–Book 5 of the Badger Hills Farm series by Jenny Phillips.

Available at
goodandbeautiful.com

MORE BOOKS FROM
THE GOOD AND THE BEAUTIFUL

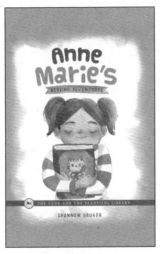

*Anne Marie's
Reading Adventures*
By Shannen Yauger

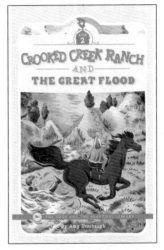

*Crooked Creek Ranch
and The Great Flood*
By Amy Drorbaugh